Let's play Jazz!

I want to play Jazz on the **trumpet**.

Well known classic Jazz Trumpeters:
Louis Armstrong, Miles Davis, Chet Baker,
Dizzy Gillespie and many more...

I want to play Jazz on the **guitar**.

Well known classic Jazz Guitarists:
Django Reinhardt, Wes Montgomery, Charlie Christian, George Benson and many more...

I want to play Jazz on the **saxophone**.

Well known classic Jazz Saxophonists:
John Coltrane, Charlie Parker, Coleman Hawkins, Lester Young and many more...

I want to play Jazz on the **drums**.

Well known classic Jazz Drummers: Art Blakey, Tony Williams, Kenny Clarke, Max Roach and many more...

I want to play Jazz on the **piano**.

Well known classic Jazz Pianists: Thelonious Monk, Bill Evans, Duke Ellington, Oscar Peterson and many more...

I want to play Jazz on the **bass**.

Well known classic Jazz Bassists: Charles Mingus, Jaco Pastorius, Paul Chambers, Ray Brown, Sam Jones and many more...

I want to play Jazz on the **trombone**.

Well known classic Jazz Trombonists: Jack Teagarden, J. J. Johnson, Glenn Miller, Tommy Dorsey, and many more...

I want to play Jazz on the **clarinet**.

Well known classic Jazz Clarinet Players: Benny Goodman, Sidney Bechet, Johnny Dodds, Artie Shaw, and many more...

trumpet

guitar

saxophone

drums

piano

bass

trombone

clarinet

Would you like to play Jazz?

www.ingramcontent.com/pod-product-compliance
Lightning Source LLC
Chambersburg PA
CBHW061318040426
42444CB00010B/2694